"I have a dream that one day this nation will rise up and live out the true meaning of its creed: 'We hold this to be self-evident, that all men are created equal.'"
—MARTIN LUTHER KING JR., AUGUST 28, 1963

MARTIN LUTHER KING JR.: CIVIL RIGHTS LEADER AND NOBEL PRIZE WINNER

BY ANDREW SANTELLA

Content Reviewer: Susan Englander, Ph.D., Assistant Editor,
Martin Luther King, Jr. Papers Project at Stanford University

The Child's World

Published in the United States of America by The Child's World®
PO Box 326
Chanhassen, MN 55317-0326
800-599-READ
www.childsworld.com

The Child's World®: Mary Berendes, Publishing Director
Editorial Directions, Inc.: E. Russell Primm and Emily Dolbear, Editors; Katie Marsico and
Elizabeth K. Martin, Editorial Assistants; Dawn Friedman, Photo Researcher; Linda S. Koutris,
Photo Selector; Kerry Reid, Fact Researcher; Susan Hindman, Copy Editor; Halley Gatenby,
Proofreader; Tim Griffin/IndexServ, Indexer; Vicki Fischman, Page Production

Cover photograph: Martin Luther King Jr. at a press conference in Montgomery, Alabama,
on March 12, 1965 / © Corbis

Interior photographs ©: Cover: Bettman/Corbis; AP/Wide World Photos: 9, 13, 14, 30, 31, 35; Gene
Herrick/AP/Wide World Photos: 20; Bill Hudson/AP/Wide World Photos: 29; Flip Schulke/Corbis: 6, 15, 23,
25, 36; Bettmann/Corbis: 2, 8, 12, 16, 21, 26, 27, 28, 32, 34; Jack Moebes/Corbis: 24; Hulton Archive/Getty
Images: 19; Library of Congress: 10; Herman Hiller/New York World-Telegram and the Sun Newspaper
Photograph Collection/ Library of Congress: 17.

Library of Congress Cataloging-in-Publication Data

Santella, Andrew.
Martin Luther King Jr. : civil rights leader and Nobel Prize winner /by Andrew Santella.
p. cm. — (Journey to freedom)
Includes bibliographical references and index.
Contents: The pastor's son—The education of a leader—Montgomery—A national leader—The final years.
ISBN 1-56766-539-X (lib. bdg. : alk. paper)
1. King, Martin Luther, Jr., 1929–1968—Juvenile literature. 2. African Americans–Biography—Juvenile litera-
ture. 3. Civil rights workers—United States—Biography—Juvenile literature. 4. Baptists–United States—
Clergy—Biography—Juvenile literature. 5. African Americans—Civil rights—History–20th century—Juvenile
literature. [1. King, Martin Luther, Jr., 1929–1968. 2. Civil rights workers. 3. Clergy. 4. African Americans—
Biography. 5. Nobel Prizes–Biography.] I. Title. II. Series.
E185.97.K5S25 2004
323'.092–dc21
2003004291

Contents

The March on Washington

On a steamy August day in 1963, a vast crowd gathered in front of the Lincoln Memorial in Washington, D.C. There were enough people in this one area of the nation's capitol to fill a medium-sized city. In all, about 250,000 people had made their way to the monument. They included poor farmers and college professors, ministers and movie stars. People of all backgrounds had come to Washington from every part of the country. They were there to demand freedom and justice for **African-Americans.** They called their gathering the March on Washington for Jobs and Freedom.

In many places in the United States in 1963, African-Americans were not free to live where they liked. They could not send their children to the best public schools. Unfair laws denied some blacks the right to vote.

The people gathered for the March on Washington for Jobs and Freedom were determined to end such injustice. For leadership, they looked to one man above all others. He was not a powerful politician, or a general, or the head of a huge company. He was a **pastor** at a Baptist church in Atlanta, Georgia. His name was Martin Luther King Jr.

THOUSANDS OF MARCHERS GATHER AT THE LINCOLN MEMORIAL AND ITS REFLECTING POOL FOR THE MARCH ON WASHINGTON FOR JOBS AND FREEDOM IN 1963.

For eight years, King had been leading the struggle to win basic rights for African-Americans. He had led marches and protests. He had endured violent abuse. Several times, he had been arrested and thrown in jail for demanding his rights as an American citizen. His work had made him famous all over the world. Still, King had never spoken to a crowd as large as the one gathered on August 28, 1963. People filled every inch of space on the lawn in front of the Lincoln Memorial. Thousands more around the world watched on television.

MARTIN LUTHER KING JR. ORGANIZED MANY PROTESTS IN THE 1960s. IN 1961, THE POLICE CHIEF IN ALBANY, GEORGIA, ARRESTS KING FOR NOT HAVING A PERMIT TO LEAD A PARADE.

On the speaker's platform, King began reading a speech he had written for the occasion. About halfway through his speech, he stopped reading and started speaking from his heart. He told the crowd about a dream he had. "I have a dream," he said, "that my four little children will one day live in a nation where they will not be judged by the color of their skin, but by the content of their character."

As King spoke, people in the crowd shouted out their support. Some people joined hands and swayed back and forth. King went on, "I have a dream that one day . . . little black boys and black girls will be able to join hands with little white boys and white girls as sisters and brothers."

"And when this happens," King continued, "we will be able . . . to join hands and sing in the words of the old Negro spiritual, 'Free at last! Free at last! Thank God almighty, we are free at last!'"

King did not live to see his dream come true. But his dream would live on in the hearts of the many Americans he inspired.

MARTIN LUTHER KING JR. ADDRESSES THOUSANDS OF CIVIL RIGHTS SUPPORTERS GATHERED IN FRONT OF THE LINCOLN MEMORIAL ON AUGUST 28, 1963. IT WAS A HISTORIC SPEECH.

The Pastor's Son

Martin Luther King Jr. was born Michael King Jr. in Atlanta on January 15, 1929. About five years later, both he and his father changed their names to Martin Luther King (around the house, Martin Jr. was simply called M. L.). Martin Luther was an important religious leader of the 1500s, and religion was an important part of the King household.

M. L.'s father, was the pastor of Ebenezer Baptist Church. M. L.'s grandfather on his mother's side had been pastor of the church before him. On Sundays, the entire King family spent all day at church. M. L., his sister Willie Christine, and his brother Alfred Daniel attended services and Bible study. Their mother, Alberta Williams King, played the church organ.

In many ways, M. L. had a typical childhood. He delivered newspapers to earn spending money and spent his free time flying kites and model airplanes. He loved sports, too, and especially enjoyed rough-and-tumble games of football on empty lots in his neighborhood. Even before he started school, he displayed an eagerness to read as much as he could.

MARTIN LUTHER KING WAS BORN IN THIS HOUSE IN ATLANTA, GEORGIA, ON JANUARY 15, 1929.

But all was not well in M. L.'s world. He was growing up black in a world controlled by powerful white people. This meant that M. L. could not enjoy the same rights and **privileges** as white people.

In the South, whites and African-Americans attended separate schools and churches. In public places, African-Americans had to drink from water fountains marked "colored." They used separate "colored" bathrooms in train stations and at bus depots. They swam in "colored" swimming pools if there were any available. In most aspects of everyday life, African-Americans were kept separate—or segregated—from whites. On election day, African-Americans were too often denied the voting rights that whites enjoyed. In some places, for example, blacks were unfairly required to pass reading tests or to pay taxes before voting.

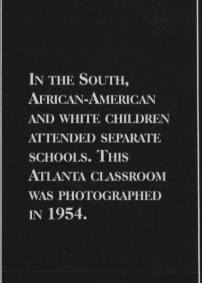

IN THE SOUTH, AFRICAN-AMERICAN AND WHITE CHILDREN ATTENDED SEPARATE SCHOOLS. THIS ATLANTA CLASSROOM WAS PHOTOGRAPHED IN 1954.

At a young age, M. L. learned about the unfairness of **segregation**. In preschool, one of his playmates was a white boy. When the time came for the two boys to start elementary school, they had to enroll in separate schools. What's more, the white boy's parents decided that their son should no longer play with M. L. The reason was simple. Their son was white. And M. L. was black.

Not surprising, this decision hurt and disturbed young M. L. His mother gave him some advice that stayed with him for the rest of his life. M. L.'s father later remembered his wife's words as "Never think, son, that there is anything that makes a person *better* than you are, especially the color of his skin."

M. L.'s MOTHER, ALBERTA WILLIAMS KING, IN THIS UNDATED PHOTOGRAPH

The Education of a Leader

Young M. L. grew up quickly. At six years old, he was singing church hymns with his mother in front of audiences. At 13, he entered Booker T. Washington High School in Atlanta. When he was just 15 years old, he passed the college entrance exams that allowed him to enroll at Morehouse College in Atlanta.

Morehouse had started a special program that allowed gifted younger students to begin college early. High school–age students like M. L. could take the place of college students who had gone off to fight in World War II. Morehouse was a natural choice for M. L. Both his father and his mother's father had attended the school. M. L. lived at home while he attended college, and he concentrated on his studies. He received good grades, especially in English and social science.

KING, SEATED LEFT, LISTENS TO A LECTURE AT MOREHOUSE COLLEGE.

As he neared graduation, M. L. tried to decide on a career path. He was interested in medicine and in the law, but finally he decided on another profession: his father's. He would become a minister. No one was more pleased with the decision than Martin Sr. In February 1948, M. L. was **ordained** a Baptist minister, and he graduated from Morehouse that spring.

The young minister left Atlanta in 1948, having decided to work toward a bachelor of divinity degree at Crozer Theological **Seminary** in Chester, Pennsylvania. This experience was his first chance to attend a school with both white and African-American students. King involved himself deeply in campus life, and he served as president of the senior class.

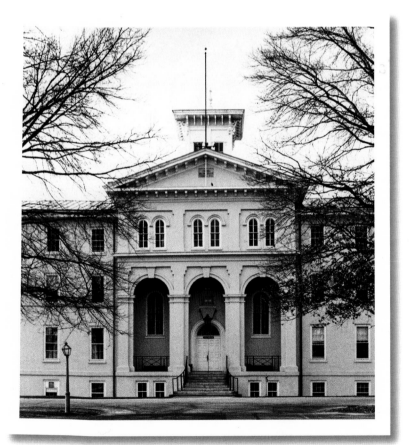

MARTIN LUTHER KING JR. LIVED IN THIS DORMITORY AS HE STUDIED FOR HIS DEGREE FROM CROZER THEOLOGICAL SEMINARY IN CHESTER, PENNSYLVANIA.

It may have been at Crozer King first learned about the ideas of Indian leader Mohandas Gandhi. Using marches, strikes, and other peaceful methods, Gandhi had led the struggle for India's independence from Great Britain. King was fascinated by Gandhi's **philosophy,** and he read everything he could about his life and work. Gandhi's ideas and accomplishments later served as the model for King's work in the United States.

MOHANDAS GANDHI WAS A FAMOUS INDIAN LEADER WHOSE PEACEFUL BELIEFS GREATLY INFLUENCED KING. GANDHI WAS SHOT AND KILLED ON JANUARY 30, 1948.

King finished his studies at Crozer at the top of his class. He was chosen to give a speech at his graduation and won a **scholarship** to pay for further study. He used the money to enroll in Boston University's School of Theology, where he began working toward a doctorate—the most advanced degree in higher education.

In Boston, he also met a music student named Coretta Scott. She was studying at a nearby music school, and the two began dating. They quickly fell in love. The couple was married on June 18, 1953, at the Scott family home in Alabama.

In the meantime, King knew exactly what he wanted to do after he finished his studies in Boston. He had decided to return to the South, where he would serve as the pastor of a church.

KING AND COR- ETTA SCOTT, SHOWN HERE IN 1964, WERE MARRIED IN 1953.

Montgomery

In 1954, Martin Luther King Jr. became pastor of Dexter Avenue Baptist Church in Montgomery, Alabama. King jumped into his new job with great energy and passion. He impressed the members of his church with his fiery sermons and his concern for the needy. He encouraged them to vote and to take part in the political life of their community. He urged them to join the National Association for the Advancement of Colored People (NAACP), which was the nation's leading **civil rights group.**

At the same time, King was completing his schooling. In 1955, he was awarded his doctorate from Boston University. The same year, Coretta gave birth to a daughter named Yolanda Denise. Then came an event that changed King's life and the lives of many Americans.

REVEREND MARTIN LUTHER KING JR. BECAME PASTOR OF DEXTER AVENUE BAPTIST CHURCH IN MONTGOMERY, ALABAMA, IN 1954.

On December 1, 1955, an African-American woman named Rosa Parks stepped on board a Montgomery bus on her way from work. Parks refused to give up her seat to a white passenger. In Montgomery, a law required that African-Americans give up their seats to whites if the buses were full. Parks was arrested and thrown in jail.

Her arrest outraged African-Americans in Montgomery. Some decided to organize a **boycott** of the Montgomery buses, and they chose King as their leader. They hoped that by refusing to ride the buses, they would pressure the city into improving the way it treated African-Americans.

King kept busy by speaking and encouraging car pools for blacks to get around. "We have no alternative but to protest," King told supporters in Montgomery. However, he insisted that the protest be a peaceful one. "We must meet the forces of hate with the power of love," he said, repeating Gandhi's words.

ROSA PARKS, SHOWN HERE BEING FINGERPRINTED, WAS ARRESTED FOR REFUSING TO GIVE UP HER SEAT TO A WHITE PASSENGER ON A MONTGOMERY BUS IN 1956.

The forces of hate were not easily defeated. On January 30, 1956, someone placed a bomb on the front porch of King's home. It exploded and broke the windows of the house, but no one was hurt. By threatening King's family, somebody was trying to frighten King into giving up his protest.

It didn't work. The boycott went on for more than a year, and finally justice won out. On November 13, 1956, the U.S. Supreme Court made segregation on buses in Alabama illegal. Never again was it legal for a Montgomery bus driver to ask African-American passengers to give up their seats to white people.

THE U.S. SUPREME COURT RULED AGAINST SEGREGATION ON ALABAMA BUSES IN 1956. AFTER THE HISTORIC RULING, KING RIDES THE BUS NEXT TO GLENN SMILEY, A STRONG SUPPORTER OF THE MONTGOMERY BUS BOYCOTT.

A National Leader

The victory in Montgomery helped make King famous across the country. He formed a group called the Southern Christian Leadership Conference (SCLC) to lead the drive for civil rights in the South. His picture appeared on the cover of national magazines. He was invited to speak at colleges and churches all over the United States. However, his fame also exposed him to new dangers. On a visit to New York in 1958, he was attacked and stabbed by a disturbed woman. King recovered from the wound, but for the rest of his life he had to live with the threat of violence against him and his family.

AT AN ATLANTA RESTAURANT IN THE EARLY 1960s, MARTIN LUTHER KING JR. LISTENS DURING A STAFF MEETING OF HIS SOUTHERN CHRISTIAN LEADERSHIP CONFERENCE (SCLC).

In 1959, the Kings traveled to India, the land where Gandhi had used nonviolent protest to win his people's freedom. In India, King met with Gandhi's followers and was inspired by their determination to end injustice.

At the same time, more people in the United States were turning to nonviolent protest. In 1960, groups of students in several southern states challenged whites-only laws at lunch counters. Their protests were called **sit-ins** because the protesters refused to move from the lunch counter until they were served. The sit-ins forced more than 100 southern cities in the United States to end segregation at lunch counters.

FOUR YOUNG MEN PARTICIPATE IN A LUNCH COUNTER SIT-IN IN GREENSBORO, NORTH CAROLINA, IN 1960. SIT-INS WERE A PEACEFUL FORM OF PROTEST.

In 1960, King moved back to Atlanta and accepted his father's offer to become co-pastor at Ebenezer Baptist Church. He continued to support sit-ins and other forms of peaceful protest. But African-Americans in the South still had to live with segregation and **discrimination.**

One of the toughest places to be an African-American was Birmingham, Alabama. Public facilities there were segregated, and local merchants rarely hired black workers. The city's commissioner of public safety, T. Eugene "Bull" Connor, and his police treated African-Americans brutally.

In 1963, King and the SCLC set their sights on Birmingham. "We felt if we could crack that city, we could crack any city," he said later.

T. EUGENE "BULL" CONNOR, BIRMINGHAM'S COMMISSIONER OF PUBLIC SAFETY, WAS A CONTROVERSIAL CHARACTER WHOSE POLICE OFFICERS TREATED THE CITY'S AFRICAN-AMERICANS WITH BRUTALITY.

King was arrested for leading a march demanding an end to segregation in Birmingham. While he sat in his Birmingham jail cell, he wrote a letter explaining the principles of nonviolent protest. "There are two types of laws: just and unjust," King wrote. "I would be the first to advocate obeying just laws . . . [but] one has a moral responsibility to disobey unjust laws." King's "Letter from Birmingham Jail" was quickly published as a pamphlet, and more than one million people read it.

MARTIN LUTHER KING JR. SITS IN A JAIL CELL IN THE JEFFERSON COUNTY COURTHOUSE IN BIRMINGHAM, ALABAMA. DURING HIS TIME THERE, HE WROTE "LETTER FROM BIRMINGHAM JAIL."

THREE DEMONSTRATORS JOIN HANDS AGAINST THE FORCE OF WATER SPRAYED
BY POLICE IN BIRMINGHAM, ALABAMA, DURING THE PROTESTS IN 1963.

Meanwhile, the protests in Birmingham continued, and even high school and grade school children joined in. Police turned high-pressure water hoses on young demonstrators and allowed attack dogs to bite some of them. Images of the police tactics appeared on national television and in newspapers, shocking the nation. Upon his release from jail, King asserted that the eyes of the world were watching Birmingham.

The events in Birmingham helped push the nation's leaders into action. That year, President John F. Kennedy proposed legislation outlawing segregation in public facilities.

A POLICE DOG ATTACKS A YOUNG AFRICAN-AMERICAN PROTESTER IN BIRMINGHAM, ALABAMA.

To rally support for the proposed law, King organized the peaceful March on Washington for Jobs and Freedom on August 28, 1963. Before those 250,000 people who were gathered at the Lincoln Memorial, King delivered his historic "I Have a Dream" speech. He said his goal was "to arouse the conscience of the nation." He succeeded.

MARTIN LUTHER KING JR., THIRD FROM LEFT, MARCHES WITH ARMS LINKED DURING THE MARCH ON WASHINGTON FOR JOBS AND FREEDOM ON AUGUST 28, 1963.

Congress soon passed the Civil Rights Act of 1964, which outlawed discrimination in the workplace, schools, and in public places. For his part in making the law a reality and for his practice of nonviolent protest, King was awarded the Nobel Peace Prize later that year. The prestigious prize honors the person who does the best work to promote international peace during the previous year. At 35, King was the youngest person ever to receive a Nobel Prize.

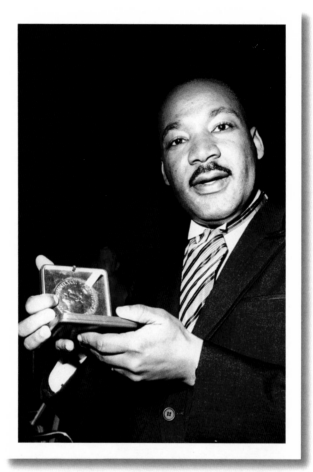

MARTIN LUTHER KING JR. POSES FOR A PHOTOGRAPH HOLDING HIS NOBEL PEACE PRIZE MEDAL ON DECEMBER 10, 1964.

IN 1965, MARTIN LUTHER KING JR. ADDRESSES A HUGE GATHERING IN SELMA, ALABAMA. KING AND HIS FOLLOWERS WERE PROTESTING UNFAIR VOTING RULES.

The Final Years

The Civil Rights Act was a great step forward for racial equality. King knew, however, that there was still more work to do. One of his goals was to increase the number of African-American voters. In many places, unfair laws still kept some African-Americans from voting in elections.

In Selma, Alabama, only a few hundred of 15,000 African-Americans were registered to vote. In 1965, King led hundreds of African-Americans in marches to the Selma courthouse, where they tried to register to vote. On February 1, 1965, King was arrested for violating the city's laws governing parades. He was released from jail after five days.

In March, a group of protesters tried to march from Selma to the state capital of Montgomery. Along the way, the march was brutally broken up by state troopers swinging billy clubs. Several weeks later, King was finally able to lead marchers to Montgomery. The protests helped win support for the Voting Rights Act of 1965. This act ensured that African-Americans would not be stopped from voting.

Of course, racial injustice was not just a southern problem. In northern cities, African-Americans often lived in poor, all-black neighborhoods, with little hope for a better life. In 1966, King went to Chicago to protest segregation in housing. He led marches in all-white neighborhoods, where African-Americans were never allowed to live. However, his protests there had little effect.

At the same time, a new generation of African-American leaders was questioning King's peaceful approach. New leaders such as Stokely Carmichael used the slogan "Black Power" and encouraged African-Americans to fight back against injustice.

King continued to preach non-violence. In 1967, he spoke out against involvement in the Vietnam War. More and more, he focused on ending poverty and unemployment, not just among African-Americans but in all communities. He began to lay plans for a massive but peaceful Poor People's March on Washington. However, his plans were interrupted by a call from Memphis, Tennessee.

Sanitation workers in Memphis were on strike to win fair wages and better working conditions. King went to Memphis to speak to the striking workers and to support them. In a speech on April 3, 1968, he urged his audience to keep working for justice and equality. "I've seen the promised land!" he declared. "I may not get there with you, but I want you to know tonight that we as a people will get to the promised land."

KING STANDS WITH LEADERS OF A SANITATION STRIKE THAT TOOK PLACE IN MEMPHIS, TENNESSEE, IN 1968.

The next day, King was relaxing on the balcony outside his Memphis motel room. Suddenly and horribly, a gunshot rang out from a building across the street. King fell, wounded in the head and neck. He was pronounced dead at a nearby hospital within an hour. He was just 39 years old.

Nearly one year later, a drifter named James Earl Ray pleaded guilty to firing the shot that killed King. He was sentenced to 99 years in prison.

CORETTA SCOTT KING, WEARING A HAT AND GLOVES, AND HER FOUR CHILDREN VIEW THE BODY OF HER HUSBAND, MARTIN LUTHER KING JR., IN ATLANTA ON APRIL 7, 1968. KING WAS SHOT AND KILLED IN MEMPHIS, TENNESSEE, ON APRIL 4, 1968.

From the mid-1950s until his death in 1968, Martin Luther King Jr. was one of the principal leaders of the movement for civil rights. Even though his life was cruelly cut short, his achievements were remarkable. He helped end the system of segregation that had made African-Americans second-class citizens. His peaceful protests called attention to injustice and **racism.** His stirring words rallied African-Americans to demand their basic rights as Americans. Those words continue to inspire people of all backgrounds.

King was buried at Southview Cemetery in Atlanta on April 9, 1968. Two years later, his body was moved to the Martin Luther King, Jr. Center for Nonviolent Social Change. Carved into the stone of his burial place were the words he had spoken at the Lincoln Memorial in 1963: "Free at Last, Free at Last/Thank God Almighty/I'm Free at Last."

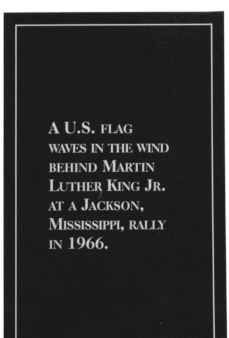

A U.S. FLAG WAVES IN THE WIND BEHIND MARTIN LUTHER KING JR. AT A JACKSON, MISSISSIPPI, RALLY IN 1966.

Timeline

1929	Martin Luther King Jr. is born on January 15 in Atlanta, Georgia.
1942	King enters Booker T. Washington High School in Atlanta.
1944	At the age of 15, King begins studying at Morehouse College in Atlanta.
1948	King is ordained a Baptist minister. He graduates from Morehouse College and goes on to Crozer Theological Seminary.
1953	King marries Coretta Scott on June 18.
1954	King becomes pastor of Dexter Avenue Baptist Church in Montgomery, Alabama.
1955	King is awarded a doctorate in theology from Boston University. He leads a boycott of the Montgomery, Alabama, bus system, after Rosa Parks refuses to give up her seat to a white passenger.
1956	King's home is bombed; no one is hurt. The Montgomery boycott continues. On November 13, the U.S. Supreme Court rules segregation on buses in Alabama is illegal.
1957	King forms a group called the Southern Christian Leadership Conference (SCLC) to lead the drive for civil rights in the South.
1958	King is attacked and stabbed by a disturbed woman on a visit to New York.
1959	The Kings travel to India, where Gandhi had used nonviolent protest to win his people's freedom.
1960	King moves back to Atlanta to become co-pastor at Ebenezer Baptist Church with his father.
1963	On August 28, some 250,000 people gather for the March on Washington for Jobs and Freedom. King gives his historic "I Have a Dream" speech at the Lincoln Memorial.
1964	King wins the Nobel Peace Prize. The U.S. Congress passes the Civil Rights Act.
1965	King leads a voting rights campaign in Selma, Alabama. Congress passes the Voting Rights Act.
1966	King goes to Chicago to protest segregation in housing.
1968	King is shot and killed in Memphis, Tennessee, on April 4. He is buried at Southview Cemetery in Atlanta on April 9.
1970	King's body is moved to the Martin Luther King, Jr. Center for Nonviolent Social Change

Glossary

**African-Americans
(AF-ri-kehn uh-MER-ih-kehnz)**
African-Americans are black Americans whose
ancestors came from Africa. Martin Luther
King Jr. is one of the world's most respected
African-Americans.

boycott (BOI-kot)
A boycott is the act of refusing to buy or use
a product or service as a protest. In 1955, King
led a boycott of the Montgomery bus system.

civil rights group (SIV-il RITES GROOP)
A civil rights group is an organization that
works to gain equal laws and equal rights
for all citizens. The National Association for
the Advancement of Colored People (NAACP)
is one of the nation's leading civil rights groups.

discrimination (diss-KRIM-uh-NAY-shun)
Discrimination is the act of treating people
unfairly based on their race, sex, or back-
ground. African-Americans faced discrimination for many years in the United States.

ordained (or-DANED)
To be ordained means to be officially appoin-
ted a minister. King was ordained a Baptist
minister in 1947.

pastor (PASS-tur)
A pastor is a minister of a church. King and
his father were both pastors.

philosophy (fuh-LOSS-uh-fee)
A philosophy is a person's basic ideas and
beliefs about how to live. Indian leader
Mohandas Gandhi's philosophies, which
were rooted in peaceful protest, greatly influenced King.

privileges (PRIV-uh-lid-jiz)
Privileges are special rights or advantages.
Growing up in the South, King did not have
the same rights and privileges as white citizens.

racism (RAY-siz-um)
Racism is the belief that one race of people is
better than another. African-Americans often
faced racism throughout the history of the
United States.

scholarship (SKOL-ur-ship)
A scholarship is a grant or a prize that pays for
college. After graduating from Crozer Theological Seminary, King won a scholarship for
further study.

segregation (seg-ruh-GAY-shuhn)
Segregation is the practice of keeping racial
groups apart. Segregation is no longer legal
in the United States.

seminary (SEM-uh-NER-ee)
A seminary is a school that trains ministers,
priests, or rabbis. King earned a bachelor of
divinity degree at Crozer Theological Seminary in Pennsylvania.

sit-ins (SIT-ins)
Sit-ins are a form of protest in which people
enter a public place and refuse to leave for a
long period of time. In 1960, students staged
sit-ins to protest segregation at lunch counters.

Index

Further Information

Books

de Kay, James T. *Meet Martin Luther King, Jr.* New York: Random House Children's Books, 1993.

Farris, Christine King, and Chris Soentpiet. *My Brother Martin.* New York: Simon & Schuster Children's Books, 2002.

Peck, Ira. *The Life and Words of Martin Luther King, Jr.* New York: Scholastic, 2000.

Pettit, Jayne. *Martin Luther King, Jr.: A Man with a Dream.* Danbury, Conn.: Scholastic Library Publishing, 2000.

Web Sites

Visit our homepage for lots of links about Martin Luther King Jr.:
http://www.childsworld.com/links.html

Note to Parents, Teachers, and Librarians:
We routinely verify our Web links to make sure they're safe,
active sites—so encourage your readers to check them out!

About the Author

Andrew Santella is the author of a number of nonfiction books for young readers. He also writes regularly for publications ranging from the *New York Times Book Review* to *GQ.* He is a graduate of Loyola University in Chicago.

tella, Andrew.

in Luther King